"Wealth Mastery Unleashed: Uncover the Life Insurance Blueprint to Generational Prosperity"

I. Introduction

I0446179

A. Understanding the importance of generational wealth for breaking the cycle of poverty

Generational wealth refers to the assets, resources, and financial stability that are passed down from one generation to another within a family. It plays a crucial role in breaking the cycle of poverty by providing opportunities and advantages to future generations.

One key aspect of generational wealth is the ability to invest in education. With financial stability, families can afford quality education for their children, which can lead to better job opportunities and higher income levels in the future. Education equips individuals with the necessary skills and knowledge to succeed, enabling them to break free from the limitations of poverty.

Generational wealth also provides a safety net during emergencies and unexpected financial setbacks. Having assets such as savings, property, or investments allows families to weather difficult times without falling back into poverty. This stability provides a foundation for future generations to build upon and creates a sense of security that can help break the cycle of poverty.

Furthermore, generational wealth allows families to invest in entrepreneurial endeavors and create businesses. This not only

1

generates income but also creates job opportunities for others in the community. By building and growing businesses, families can contribute to economic development, which in turn can uplift the entire community and break the cycle of poverty for many individuals.

Finally, generational wealth enables families to access better healthcare, nutrition, and living conditions. Improved health outcomes and access to quality healthcare can lead to longer and more productive lives. Additionally, living in safe and stable environments can positively impact overall well-being and provide a solid foundation for future generations to thrive.

In conclusion, generational wealth is crucial for breaking the cycle of poverty as it provides opportunities for education, stability during difficult times, entrepreneurial endeavors, improved living conditions, and better access to healthcare. By accumulating and passing down assets and resources, families can create a positive trajectory for future generations, ultimately breaking free from the cycle of poverty.

B. Introducing life insurance as a powerful tool for creating and preserving wealth

Life insurance is indeed a powerful tool that can play a significant role in creating and preserving wealth for individuals and their families. While life insurance is primarily known for providing financial protection in the event of the policyholder's death, it offers several additional benefits that can contribute to long-term wealth building.

One key aspect of life insurance is its ability to provide a tax-free death benefit to beneficiaries. This benefit ensures that loved ones are financially protected and can maintain their standard of living even after the policyholder's passing. By receiving a lump sum payout, beneficiaries can use the funds to pay off debts, cover funeral expenses, and replace lost income. This financial security helps preserve existing wealth and provides a foundation for future financial endeavors.

Moreover, certain types of life insurance, such as whole life or universal life insurance, offer a cash value component. As policyholders pay their premiums, a portion of each payment goes towards accumulating cash value over time. This cash value grows tax-deferred and can be accessed during the policyholder's lifetime through policy loans or withdrawals. These funds can be used for various purposes, such as supplementing retirement income, funding education expenses, or even starting a business. The ability to access accumulated cash value provides a valuable asset that can contribute to wealth creation and preservation.

Additionally, life insurance can be utilized as an estate planning tool. By naming beneficiaries, policyholders can ensure a smooth transfer of wealth to their loved ones upon their death, bypassing the probate process. This can help preserve the value of the estate and minimize potential estate taxes, allowing more wealth to be passed on to future generations.

Furthermore, life insurance can be used as collateral for loans or as a means of protecting business interests. Policyholders can assign their life insurance policy as collateral for loans, which can help secure favorable interest rates and terms. Additionally, business owners can utilize life insurance to fund buy-sell agreements, ensuring a smooth transition of ownership in case of the death of a business partner.

In summary, life insurance is a powerful tool for creating and preserving wealth. It provides a tax-free death benefit to protect loved ones, offers a cash value component for financial flexibility, aids in estate planning, and can be used as collateral for loans or to protect business interests. By integrating life insurance into a comprehensive financial plan, individuals can leverage its benefits to build and preserve wealth for themselves and future generations.

C. Purpose of the book: Empowering the underprivileged with

knowledge and strategies to leverage life insurance for long-term financial security

The purpose of the book is to empower the underprivileged with knowledge and strategies to leverage life insurance for long-term financial security. It aims to provide individuals who may not have had access to financial education with the necessary information to make informed decisions about life insurance and its potential benefits.

By offering practical guidance and insights, the book seeks to break down complex concepts and make them accessible to a wider audience. It aims to educate readers about the various types of life insurance policies available, their features, and how they can be utilized to create a solid foundation for financial stability.

The book also aims to highlight the importance of long-term financial planning and the role that life insurance can play in building and preserving wealth. It may explore topics such as the benefits of starting early, understanding policy terms and conditions, and maximizing the value of life insurance through proper coverage and policy management.

Furthermore, the book may address specific challenges and considerations faced by the underprivileged when it comes to accessing life insurance. It may discuss strategies for overcoming financial barriers, such as affordable premium options, government assistance programs, or community resources that can help individuals obtain and maintain life insurance coverage.

Overall, the purpose of the book is to empower the underprivileged by equipping them with the knowledge and strategies needed to leverage life insurance as a tool for long-term financial security. It seeks to level the playing field and provide individuals from all walks of life with the information and resources necessary to make informed decisions about their financial future.

II. The Foundations of Generational Wealth

A. Exploring the benefits of building wealth across generations

Exploring the benefits of building wealth across generations can have a profound impact on individuals and families. Here are some key advantages to consider:

1. Financial Security: Building wealth across generations provides a safety net for future generations. It allows families to weather unexpected financial challenges, such as medical expenses, job loss, or economic downturns. By creating a solid financial foundation, families can navigate difficult times with greater resilience.

2. Education and Opportunities: Accumulating wealth over time enables families to invest in education and provide opportunities for their children and grandchildren. It can fund quality education, vocational training, or entrepreneurship ventures, opening doors to higher-paying jobs and increased social mobility.

3. Legacy and Values: Building wealth across generations allows families to pass down their values, traditions, and knowledge along with their financial assets. It creates a legacy that extends beyond monetary wealth, emphasizing the importance of hard work, discipline, and responsibility.

4. Philanthropy and Giving Back: Wealth that is built over generations provides the means for families to contribute to charitable causes and make a positive impact on society. It allows for philanthropic endeavors, supporting causes that align with the family's values and passions.

5. Financial Independence: Wealth built across generations can lead to financial independence for future generations. It reduces

the reliance on external sources of income and creates a sense of security and freedom to pursue personal and professional goals without financial constraints.

6. Multi-generational Collaboration: Building wealth across generations encourages collaboration and communication within the family. It fosters a sense of shared responsibility and helps family members learn from one another's experiences and expertise.

7. Long-Term Planning: Building wealth across generations requires long-term planning and strategic decision-making. This cultivates financial discipline and a forward-thinking mindset, enabling families to make informed choices that lead to sustained wealth creation.

By exploring and embracing the benefits of building wealth across generations, families can create a lasting legacy that goes beyond their immediate financial well-being. It provides a platform for future generations to thrive, fostering stability, opportunity, and a sense of purpose.

B. Identifying the obstacles faced by the poor in wealth creation

Identifying the obstacles faced by the poor in wealth creation is crucial for understanding and addressing the root causes of economic inequality. Here are some common obstacles that the poor often encounter:

1. Limited access to education and skills development: Lack of quality education and training opportunities can hinder the poor from acquiring the necessary skills and knowledge to secure higher-paying jobs or start their own businesses. This limits their ability to generate income and accumulate wealth.

2. Lack of capital and financial resources: The poor often face difficulties in accessing capital and financial resources to invest in

income-generating activities. They may struggle to obtain loans, have limited savings, or lack access to banking services, which can impede their ability to start or expand businesses.

3. Limited employment opportunities: The poor may face a scarcity of formal employment opportunities in their communities. This can result in lower wages, unstable income, and limited prospects for career advancement, making it challenging to build wealth over time.

4. Systemic barriers and discrimination: Discrimination based on factors such as gender, race, ethnicity, or socioeconomic status can create additional obstacles for the poor. It can limit their access to resources, job opportunities, credit, and social networks necessary for wealth creation.

5. Lack of financial literacy and awareness: Limited knowledge about financial management, investment strategies, and entrepreneurship can hinder the poor from making informed decisions about their finances. This can lead to poor financial choices, vulnerability to scams, and missed opportunities for wealth accumulation.

6. Inadequate social safety nets: Insufficient social protection measures, such as healthcare, unemployment benefits, or retirement plans, can leave the poor vulnerable to economic shocks and setbacks. Without adequate support, it becomes challenging to break free from the cycle of poverty and build wealth.

7. Limited social and professional networks: The poor often face challenges in establishing supportive networks that can provide access to job opportunities, mentorship, and business connections. Lack of connections can limit their ability to access resources and opportunities for wealth creation.

Addressing these obstacles requires a multi-faceted approach that focuses on improving access to quality education, promoting financial inclusion, creating employment opportunities, addressing systemic discrimination, and implementing robust social safety nets. Additionally, providing financial literacy programs and fostering supportive networks can empower the poor to navigate the challenges of wealth creation and achieve long-term economic stability.

C. Highlighting the role of life insurance in overcoming these challenges

Life insurance can play a significant role in helping individuals overcome some of the challenges they face in wealth creation. Here's how life insurance can be beneficial:

1. Financial protection for families: Life insurance provides a safety net for families in the event of the policyholder's death. It ensures that dependents are financially protected and can continue their lives without facing significant financial hardships. This protection allows families to maintain their standard of living, pay off debts, cover funeral expenses, and meet other financial obligations.

2. Income replacement: For individuals who are the primary breadwinners, life insurance can replace lost income and provide a source of financial stability for their families. This can help bridge the gap between the loss of income and finding alternative means of support, thus preventing a sudden decline in the family's financial well-being.

3. Debt management: Life insurance proceeds can be used to pay off outstanding debts such as mortgages, loans, or credit card balances. By eliminating or reducing debt obligations, life insurance can alleviate financial burdens and provide a fresh start for families or individuals, allowing them to focus on wealth creation and financial stability.

4. Legacy planning: Life insurance can be used as a tool for creating a financial legacy. Policyholders can designate

beneficiaries and leave behind a lump sum or regular income to secure the financial future of their loved ones. This can help bridge the wealth gap and provide opportunities for the next generation to pursue education, start businesses, or invest in wealth-building activities.

5. Business continuity: For entrepreneurs or small business owners, life insurance can ensure the continuity of their business in the event of their death. The proceeds from a life insurance policy can be used to cover operational expenses, repay business loans, or provide funds for a smooth transition of ownership. This protects the business and its employees, allowing it to continue generating income and contributing to wealth creation.

6. Estate planning and tax benefits: Life insurance can be an effective tool for estate planning, helping individuals pass on their wealth to future generations. Life insurance proceeds are generally tax-free, which means beneficiaries receive the full benefit amount without incurring significant tax liabilities. This can help protect the wealth accumulated over a lifetime and ensure its efficient transfer to heirs.

It's important to note that life insurance should be considered as part of a broader financial plan that addresses the specific needs and goals of individuals or families. Consulting with a financial advisor can provide guidance on selecting the right type and amount of life insurance coverage to overcome the challenges faced in wealth creation.

III. Life Insurance Basics

A. Demystifying life insurance and its different types (term, whole life, indexed universal life)

Let's demystify life insurance and explore its different types:

1. Term Life Insurance: Term life insurance provides coverage for

a specific period, typically 10, 20, or 30 years. It offers a death benefit to beneficiaries if the policyholder passes away during the term. Term life insurance is generally more affordable compared to other types of life insurance, making it suitable for individuals with temporary financial obligations, such as mortgage payments or education expenses. However, it does not accumulate cash value and expires at the end of the term unless renewed.

2. Whole Life Insurance: Whole life insurance provides coverage for the entire lifetime of the insured individual. It offers a death benefit to beneficiaries and also accumulates cash value over time. Premiums for whole life insurance are typically higher than term life insurance but remain level throughout the policyholder's life. The cash value can be accessed through withdrawals or loans, providing a potential source of funds for emergencies or other financial needs.

3. Indexed Universal Life Insurance (IUL): Indexed Universal Life insurance is a type of permanent life insurance that combines a death benefit with a cash value component. The cash value of an IUL policy is linked to the performance of a specific stock market index, such as the S&P 500. This allows the policyholder to potentially earn interest based on the market's performance while also providing downside protection against market losses. IUL policies offer flexibility in premium payments and potential tax advantages, making them suitable for individuals looking for long-term coverage and potential growth of their policy's cash value.

It's important to note that the suitability of each type of life insurance depends on individual circumstances, financial goals, and risk tolerance. Consider factors such as your budget, age, health, and future financial obligations when choosing the right type of life insurance. Consulting with a licensed insurance professional or financial advisor can help you understand the nuances of each type and make an informed decision.

Remember, life insurance is designed to provide financial protection and support for your loved ones in the event of your passing. It's wise to review your policy periodically to ensure it aligns with your changing needs and goals.

B. Understanding the components of a life insurance policy and their implications

1. Death Benefit: The death benefit is the amount of money that will be paid to the beneficiaries upon the insured person's death. It is the primary purpose of life insurance and is typically tax-free. The death benefit amount is determined when purchasing the policy and should be sufficient to meet the financial needs of your loved ones in your absence.

2. Premiums: Premiums are the regular payments you make to keep the life insurance policy active. The amount of premiums depends on various factors such as your age, health, coverage amount, and type of policy. It's important to pay premiums on time to ensure continuous coverage.

3. Cash Value: Cash value is a feature found in permanent life insurance policies (such as whole life or universal life) and represents the savings component of the policy. A portion of each premium payment goes towards building the cash value over time. The cash value grows tax-deferred and can be accessed through withdrawals or loans, providing a potential source of funds for emergencies or other financial needs.

4. Policy Riders: Riders are optional add-ons to a life insurance policy that provide additional benefits or customization. Common riders include accelerated death benefit riders (allowing the policyholder to access a portion of the death benefit if diagnosed with a terminal illness), disability income riders (providing income if the policyholder becomes disabled), or a guaranteed insurability rider (allowing the purchase of additional coverage without a medical exam).

5. Policy Exclusions: Life insurance policies may have certain exclusions or limitations. For example, suicide within a specific period after policy issuance may not be covered. It's important to review and understand these exclusions to avoid any surprises in the future.

6. Policy Terms: Policy terms include the length of coverage (in the case of term life insurance), the duration of premium payments, and any renewal or conversion options. Understanding the policy terms is vital to ensure the policy meets your long-term needs and goals.

It's essential to review and understand all the components of a life insurance policy before purchasing one. Consider your financial situation, goals, and the needs of your loved ones to make an informed decision. If you have any doubts or questions, consulting with a licensed insurance professional or financial advisor is always recommended.

C. Dispelling myths and misconceptions surrounding life insurance for the poor

There are several myths and misconceptions surrounding life insurance for the poor that need to be dispelled. Here are some common ones:

1. Myth: Life insurance is only for the wealthy.
Reality: Life insurance is not limited to the wealthy. In fact, life insurance can be an essential financial tool for individuals with limited means. It provides a way to protect their families from financial hardships in the event of their death.

2. Myth: Life insurance is too expensive for the poor.
Reality: While some types of life insurance can be costly, there are affordable options available. Term life insurance, for example, offers coverage for a specific period at lower premiums. It can be a suitable choice for those on a tight budget.

3. Myth: Poor individuals don't need life insurance.

Reality: Everyone, regardless of their financial status, can benefit from life insurance. Even if a person has limited income, life insurance can provide financial security and peace of mind. It can help cover final expenses, outstanding debts, and ensure their loved ones are taken care of.

4. Myth: Poor individuals won't qualify for life insurance due to health issues.

Reality: While poor health may impact the availability and cost of certain types of life insurance, it doesn't mean that coverage is impossible. Some policies, like guaranteed issue life insurance, don't require a medical exam or health questions. These policies may have higher premiums, but they can still offer coverage for those with health challenges.

5. Myth: Life insurance payouts will affect eligibility for government assistance programs.

Reality: In many cases, life insurance payouts are not considered income and do not affect eligibility for government assistance programs like Medicaid or Supplemental Security Income (SSI). However, it's essential to understand the rules specific to each program and seek guidance from a professional if you have concerns.

6. Myth: Life insurance for the poor is not a good investment.

Reality: While life insurance primarily provides financial protection, some policies, like permanent life insurance, can accumulate cash value over time. This cash value can be accessed if needed or used as a savings or investment tool.

It's important to dispel these myths and misconceptions surrounding life insurance for the poor. Everyone deserves the opportunity to protect their loved ones and provide financial security, regardless of their income level. Consulting with a knowledgeable insurance professional can help determine the best options within one's means.

IV. Leveraging Life Insurance for Wealth Accumulation

A. Explaining how life insurance can serve as a financial resource and asset

Life insurance can serve as a valuable financial resource and asset in several ways:

1. Protection for loved ones: The primary purpose of life insurance is to provide financial protection for your loved ones in the event of your death. The payout, known as the death benefit, can help replace lost income, cover daily living expenses, pay off debts, and fund future expenses such as education or retirement.

2. Estate planning: Life insurance can be an essential tool in estate planning. It can provide liquidity to cover estate taxes, ensuring that your assets can be passed on to your beneficiaries without them having to sell off valuable assets, such as a family home or business.

3. Business continuity: For business owners, life insurance can play a vital role in ensuring the continuity of the business in the event of the owner's death. It can provide funds to cover business expenses, repay business debts, and facilitate the smooth transfer of ownership.

4. Supplemental retirement income: Some types of life insurance, such as permanent life insurance, have a cash value component that grows over time. This cash value can be accessed during your lifetime through policy loans or withdrawals. It can serve as a supplemental source of income during retirement or in times of financial need.

5. Loan collateral: Life insurance policies with cash value can be used as collateral for loans. This can provide you with access

to funds at lower interest rates compared to other forms of borrowing.

6. Wealth transfer and charitable giving: Life insurance can be used as a tool for wealth transfer to future generations. By designating beneficiaries, you can ensure that your loved ones receive a tax-free inheritance. Additionally, life insurance can be used for charitable giving, allowing you to leave a lasting legacy and support causes you care about.

It's important to note that the specific benefits and uses of life insurance may vary depending on the type of policy and your individual circumstances. Consulting with a financial advisor or insurance professional can help you determine the best way to maximize the financial benefits of life insurance based on your goals and needs.

B. Utilizing life insurance policies as savings vehicles with cash value growth potential

Some types of life insurance, such as permanent life insurance, can serve as savings vehicles with cash value growth potential. Here's how it works:

1. Cash value accumulation: Permanent life insurance policies, such as whole life or universal life insurance, have a cash value component. A portion of the premium you pay goes towards building this cash value over time. The cash value grows on a tax-deferred basis, meaning you don't pay taxes on the growth until you withdraw or borrow against it.

2. Guaranteed growth: With certain types of permanent life insurance, there is a guaranteed minimum growth rate for the cash value component. This means that even if the market performs poorly, your cash value will still grow at a predetermined rate.

3. Flexibility in accessing funds: The cash value in your life

insurance policy can be accessed in several ways. You can take out a policy loan against the cash value, which you'll need to pay back with interest. Alternatively, you can make partial withdrawals from the cash value, reducing the death benefit accordingly. These withdrawals are generally tax-free up to the amount you've paid in premiums. However, if you surrender the policy entirely, taxes may apply to any gain in the cash value.

4. Potential for dividends: Some permanent life insurance policies, such as participating whole life insurance, may pay dividends to policyholders. These dividends are a portion of the insurer's profits and can enhance the cash value growth of the policy. Dividends can be used to increase the cash value, pay premiums, or be received as cash.

5. Estate planning advantages: The cash value in a life insurance policy can be passed on to your beneficiaries tax-free upon your death. This can be a useful tool for estate planning, providing a tax-efficient way to transfer wealth to the next generation.

It's important to note that using life insurance as a savings vehicle requires a long-term commitment, as it typically takes several years for the cash value to accumulate. Additionally, policy loans and withdrawals can affect the death benefit and ongoing policy performance. Consulting with a financial advisor or insurance professional can help you assess whether utilizing a life insurance policy as a savings vehicle is suitable for your financial goals and circumstances.

C. Strategies for maximizing the wealth-building potential of life insurance, tailored to the needs of the poor

When it comes to maximizing the wealth-building potential of life insurance for individuals with limited financial resources, there are a few strategies that can be tailored to their needs. Here are some suggestions:

1. Term life insurance: While permanent life insurance policies

offer cash value growth potential, they can be more expensive. For those with limited income, term life insurance can be a more affordable option. Term policies provide coverage for a specific period, such as 10, 20, or 30 years, without a cash value component. This allows individuals to prioritize protection for their loved ones at a lower cost.

2. Seek simplified issue policies: Traditional life insurance policies require a medical exam, which can be a barrier for those with limited access to healthcare or pre-existing conditions. Simplified issue policies, on the other hand, have a simplified underwriting process that doesn't require a medical exam. While they may have higher premiums, they provide an opportunity for individuals who may not qualify for traditional policies to obtain life insurance coverage.

3. Choose a policy with flexible premiums: Some life insurance policies allow for flexible premium payments. This can be useful for individuals with fluctuating incomes or irregular cash flow. They can adjust their premium payments according to their financial situation, ensuring they can maintain their coverage without straining their budget.

4. Utilize government assistance programs: Depending on the country and region, there may be government assistance programs that provide life insurance coverage for low-income individuals. Exploring these programs can be beneficial for those seeking life insurance but facing financial limitations.

5. Education and financial literacy: Empowering individuals with financial knowledge and literacy is crucial. Providing resources and education on the importance of life insurance, budgeting, and financial planning can help them make informed decisions and maximize the benefits of their policies.

Remember, while life insurance can be a valuable tool for wealth-building, it's essential to assess individual circumstances and consult with a financial advisor or insurance professional who can provide personalized guidance based on specific needs and goals.

V. Creating a Financial Blueprint

A. Assessing individual financial goals and determining the appropriate life insurance coverage

Assessing individual financial goals and determining the appropriate life insurance coverage requires careful consideration of various factors. Here are some steps to help with this process:

1. Evaluate financial responsibilities: Start by identifying your financial responsibilities, such as mortgage or rent payments, outstanding debts (like student loans or credit card debt), and ongoing living expenses. This evaluation will help you understand the financial impact your absence would have on your loved ones.

2. Consider income replacement needs: Determine how much income would need to be replaced to support your family's lifestyle in case of your untimely death. A general rule of thumb is to multiply your annual income by a factor of 5 to 10, depending on individual circumstances.

3. Factor in future financial obligations: Consider any future financial obligations, such as college tuition for children or other long-term financial goals. Including these expenses in your coverage can help ensure your loved ones are protected in the long run.

4. Assess existing assets and savings: Evaluate the assets and savings you already have, such as investments, retirement accounts, and emergency funds. These can help determine how much life insurance coverage is needed to bridge the gap between your existing resources and your financial goals.

5. Review existing life insurance coverage: If you already have life

insurance, review your current coverage to ensure it aligns with your current financial situation and goals. Evaluate whether it provides sufficient coverage or if adjustments need to be made.

6. Seek professional advice: Consult with a financial advisor or insurance professional who can provide personalized guidance based on your specific needs and goals. They can help you navigate through the various types of life insurance policies and recommend suitable coverage amounts.

Remember, life insurance needs can change over time as your financial situation evolves. Regularly reassessing your coverage and adjusting it accordingly is essential to ensure adequate protection for your loved ones.

B. Integrating life insurance into a comprehensive financial plan for generational wealth

Integrating life insurance into a comprehensive financial plan for generational wealth can be a strategic and effective approach. Here are some key considerations to keep in mind:

1. Estate planning: Life insurance can play a crucial role in estate planning by providing financial security and liquidity. It can help cover estate taxes, debts, and other expenses, allowing the transfer of assets to the next generation without depleting them.

2. Wealth transfer: Life insurance can be used as a tool for transferring wealth to future generations. By designating beneficiaries, you can ensure that the proceeds from the policy go directly to your chosen heirs. This can provide a tax-efficient way to pass on assets and create a lasting legacy.

3. Charitable giving: If philanthropy is an important part of your financial plan, life insurance can be used to support charitable causes. By naming a charitable organization as a beneficiary, you can leave a lasting impact on the causes you care about.

4. Business succession planning: If you own a business, life

insurance can be integrated into your succession plan. It can provide funds for a smooth transition of ownership and help cover any financial obligations or buyout arrangements.

5. Long-term care planning: Some life insurance policies offer riders or provisions that provide coverage for long-term care expenses. This can be valuable in preserving generational wealth by protecting assets from being depleted due to unexpected medical costs.

6. Consult with professionals: To effectively integrate life insurance into your comprehensive financial plan, it's important to consult with professionals such as financial advisors, estate planners, and insurance experts. They can help you analyze your specific goals, financial situation, and needs, and recommend the most suitable life insurance solutions.

Remember, integrating life insurance into a comprehensive financial plan requires a holistic approach and consideration of your unique circumstances. Regularly reviewing and updating your plan as your financial situation evolves is crucial to ensure that it aligns with your long-term generational wealth goals.

C. Tips for budgeting, saving, and investing to further enhance financial stability and growth

Here are some tips to help you with budgeting, saving, and investing to enhance your financial stability and growth:

1. Create a budget: Start by tracking your income and expenses to get a clear picture of your financial situation. Categorize your expenses and identify areas where you can cut back or eliminate unnecessary spending. Set realistic goals for saving and stick to your budget.

2. Prioritize saving: Make saving a priority by setting aside a portion of your income each month. Aim to save at least 10-20% of your income, if possible. Automate your savings by setting up

automatic transfers to a separate savings account or investment vehicle.

3. Emergency fund: Build an emergency fund to cover unexpected expenses. Aim to save 3-6 months' worth of living expenses. This fund acts as a safety net and helps you avoid going into debt when faced with unexpected situations.

4. Pay off high-interest debt: Prioritize paying off high-interest debt, such as credit card balances or personal loans. By reducing or eliminating high-interest debt, you can save on interest payments and free up more money for saving and investing.

5. Diversify your investments: Don't put all your eggs in one basket. Diversify your investment portfolio by spreading your investments across different asset classes, such as stocks, bonds, real estate, and mutual funds. This helps reduce risk and increases the potential for growth.

6. Start early and be consistent: The power of compounding can significantly impact your investments over time. Start investing as early as possible and consistently contribute to your investment accounts. Regularly review and rebalance your portfolio to ensure it aligns with your long-term goals.

7. Educate yourself: Stay informed about personal finance and investment strategies. Read books, attend seminars, or follow reputable financial blogs to enhance your knowledge. Consider consulting with a financial advisor who can provide guidance tailored to your specific needs.

8. Review and adjust: Regularly review your budget, savings, and investment strategies. Life circumstances change, and so should your financial plan. Adjust your goals, strategies, and allocations as needed to stay on track and make the most of your resources.

Remember, financial stability and growth require discipline, patience, and a long-term perspective. By budgeting effectively, saving consistently, and investing wisely, you can enhance your financial well-being and work towards achieving your financial goals.

VI. Overcoming Barriers to Life Insurance Access

A. Addressing common challenges faced by the poor in obtaining life insurance coverage

Obtaining life insurance coverage can indeed be challenging for individuals facing financial difficulties. Here are some common challenges faced by the poor when it comes to life insurance and potential ways to address them:

1. Affordability: One of the main challenges is the cost of life insurance premiums. Traditional life insurance policies can be expensive, making them unaffordable for those with limited financial resources. In such cases, individuals can explore options like term life insurance, which offers coverage for a specific period at a lower cost.

2. Access to information: Lack of awareness and access to information about life insurance options can be a hurdle. Community outreach programs, educational workshops, and partnerships with non-profit organizations can help provide information and resources to underserved communities.

3. Underwriting criteria: Life insurance companies typically assess the risk associated with an individual before providing coverage. Those with pre-existing health conditions or limited medical history may struggle to meet the underwriting criteria. One possible solution is to explore simplified issue or guaranteed issue life insurance policies that have less stringent medical requirements.

4. Lack of trust: Some individuals may have a mistrust

of insurance companies or financial institutions due to past experiences or cultural factors. Building trust through transparent communication, community partnerships, and testimonials from individuals who have benefited from life insurance can help overcome this challenge.

5. Limited documentation: Life insurance applications often require documentation such as proof of income or identification. In cases where individuals lack traditional forms of documentation, insurance companies may consider alternative means to assess eligibility, such as bank statements, utility bills, or letters from employers or community leaders.

6. Language and literacy barriers: Language and literacy barriers can make it difficult for individuals to understand insurance policies and make informed decisions. Providing translated materials and offering support in multiple languages can help bridge this gap.

7. Lack of financial literacy: Limited knowledge of financial concepts and insurance products can hinder the ability to make informed decisions. Offering financial literacy programs or partnering with organizations that provide financial education can empower individuals to better understand the importance of life insurance and its benefits.

Addressing these challenges requires a collaborative effort between insurance companies, government agencies, non-profit organizations, and community leaders. By working together to increase access, knowledge, and affordability, more individuals from underserved communities can obtain the life insurance coverage they need to protect their loved ones and achieve financial security.

B. Advocating for policy changes and initiatives that promote affordable life insurance options for the underprivileged

Advocating for policy changes and initiatives that promote

affordable life insurance options for the underprivileged is crucial in ensuring financial security and protection for all individuals. Here are some key areas where policy changes and initiatives can make a difference:

1. Subsidized Premiums: Governments can consider providing subsidies or financial assistance to low-income individuals to make life insurance premiums more affordable. This can help bridge the affordability gap and ensure that those with limited financial resources can still access adequate coverage.

2. Increased Regulation: Governments can implement regulations that encourage insurance companies to offer more affordable life insurance options specifically designed for individuals with lower incomes. This could include setting maximum premium limits or requiring insurance companies to offer certain affordable policies to a broader range of individuals.

3. Simplified Underwriting: Streamlining the underwriting process for life insurance can make it easier for individuals with limited medical history or pre-existing conditions to obtain coverage. Governments can work with insurance regulators to develop policies that encourage the use of simplified underwriting procedures, reducing the barriers faced by the underprivileged.

4. Public Awareness Campaigns: Government and non-profit organizations can collaborate on public awareness campaigns to educate individuals about the importance of life insurance and the available affordable options. These campaigns can help dispel misconceptions, address concerns, and highlight the benefits of life insurance for financial security.

5. Partnerships with Non-profit Organizations: Governments and insurance companies can form partnerships with non-profit organizations that work directly with underprivileged communities. Through these partnerships, resources can be allocated to provide financial education, assistance with

insurance applications, and support in navigating the life insurance process.

6. Inclusive Policies: Insurance companies should be encouraged to develop inclusive policies that cater to the specific needs of underprivileged individuals. This could include policies with flexible payment options, lower coverage amounts, or policies that cater to specific demographic groups.

7. Collaboration with Insurance Industry: Governments can engage in dialogue with insurance industry stakeholders to encourage them to develop innovative and affordable life insurance products. This collaboration can lead to the creation of policies that are better suited to the needs and financial capabilities of the underprivileged.

Advocating for these policy changes and initiatives requires a multi-stakeholder approach, involving government entities, insurance regulators, insurance companies, non-profit organizations, and community leaders. By working together, we can create a more inclusive and affordable life insurance landscape that ensures financial protection for the underprivileged.

C. Navigating the application process and finding suitable life insurance solutions

Navigating the life insurance application process and finding suitable solutions can sometimes be overwhelming. Here are some steps to help you through the process:

1. Assess Your Needs: Determine the purpose of the life insurance coverage. Are you looking for income replacement, mortgage protection, or to provide for your family's future financial needs? Understanding your specific needs will help you choose the right type and amount of coverage.

2. Research Different Types of Life Insurance: There are various

types of life insurance, including term life, whole life, and universal life. Each has its own features, benefits, and costs. Research and compare these options to find the one that aligns with your needs and budget.

3. Evaluate Your Budget: Consider how much you can afford to pay for life insurance premiums. Evaluate your budget and determine the amount you can comfortably allocate towards coverage. This will help you narrow down your options and find affordable solutions.

4. Seek Professional Guidance: Consider consulting with a licensed insurance agent or financial advisor who specializes in life insurance. They can provide personalized guidance, help you understand the intricacies of different policies, and assist in finding suitable solutions based on your unique circumstances.

5. Compare Quotes: Obtain quotes from multiple insurance companies to compare premiums, coverage terms, and policy features. Online insurance comparison tools can be useful in this process. Ensure you understand any exclusions or limitations in the policies you are considering.

6. Review Policy Details: Carefully review the policy details, including the coverage amount, term length, premium payment frequency, and any additional riders or options. Understand the terms and conditions, as well as any potential changes in premiums over time.

7. Complete the Application: Once you've selected a suitable policy, complete the application accurately and honestly. Provide the required information, including your personal details, medical history, and lifestyle habits. Be prepared to undergo a medical examination if necessary.

8. Underwriting Process: The insurance company will assess your application and may require additional information or medical tests. Cooperate fully with this process to ensure a smooth

underwriting experience.

9. Finalize the Policy: If your application is approved, carefully review the policy documents before signing. Understand the premium payment schedule, grace periods, renewal options, and how to make a claim if needed.

Remember, finding suitable life insurance involves careful consideration of your needs, budget, and the reputation of the insurance provider. Take your time, ask questions, and seek professional advice when needed.

VII. Protecting Wealth and Ensuring a Lasting Legacy

A. Understanding the role of life insurance in estate planning and wealth transfer

Life insurance plays a crucial role in estate planning and wealth transfer. Here's how:

1. Estate Liquidity: Life insurance can provide immediate cash to cover estate taxes, debts, and other expenses upon the policyholder's death. This helps prevent the forced sale of assets or the depletion of estate funds, ensuring that the intended beneficiaries receive their inheritance intact.

2. Wealth Preservation: Life insurance can help preserve wealth for future generations. Rather than depleting assets to pay estate taxes or other obligations, a life insurance policy can provide the necessary funds, allowing the estate to pass on more wealth to beneficiaries.

3. Equalizing Inheritances: If a person intends to leave different assets or amounts to their beneficiaries, life insurance can help equalize the inheritances. For example, if one beneficiary is receiving a business, while another is receiving mainly cash, a life

insurance policy can be used to provide additional funds to the cash beneficiary, ensuring fairness in the distribution of assets.

4. Business Succession Planning: Life insurance can be a valuable tool in business succession planning. It can provide funds to buy out a deceased owner's shares, ensure continuity of the business, and provide financial support to the owner's family.

5. Charitable Giving: Life insurance allows individuals to make significant charitable contributions upon their death. By naming a charitable organization as the beneficiary or transferring a policy to a charity during their lifetime, individuals can leave a lasting legacy and support causes they care about.

6. Estate Equalization for Non-Liquid Assets: If a significant portion of an individual's assets is tied up in non-liquid assets, such as real estate or a closely held business, life insurance can provide a way to equalize inheritances among beneficiaries. The insurance proceeds can be used to provide an equitable distribution of assets to those who may not be interested or able to inherit the non-liquid assets.

It's important to work with an experienced estate planning attorney or financial advisor to integrate life insurance effectively into your estate plan. They can help assess your specific needs, explore different policy options, and ensure that your life insurance strategy aligns with your overall estate planning goals.

B. Utilizing life insurance to minimize tax implications and protect family assets

Utilizing life insurance can indeed help minimize tax implications and protect family assets. Here's how:

1. Estate Tax Planning: Life insurance proceeds are generally income tax-free to the beneficiaries. This means that the death benefit received from a life insurance policy is not subject to federal income tax. By using life insurance to cover estate taxes, it

helps protect family assets from being depleted by tax liabilities.

2. Income Tax Planning: Certain life insurance policies, such as cash value policies like whole life or universal life insurance, can accumulate cash value over time. The cash value growth is tax-deferred, meaning you won't owe income tax on the growth until you withdraw it. This can provide an additional source of tax-efficient income during retirement or other financial needs.

3. Asset Protection: Life insurance policies can provide asset protection in some instances. In many states, life insurance policies, particularly those with cash value, are protected from creditors to some extent. This means that the cash value and death benefit may be safeguarded from potential claims or lawsuits, helping to preserve assets for the family.

4. Wealth Transfer: Life insurance allows for the tax-efficient transfer of wealth to future generations. By designating beneficiaries, policyholders can ensure that their loved ones receive a financial safety net in the form of the life insurance proceeds. This can help protect family assets and provide financial security for heirs.

5. Business Protection: Life insurance can be a valuable tool for protecting family-owned businesses. In the event of the owner's death, life insurance can provide the necessary funds for the surviving family members to buy out the deceased owner's shares, ensuring the continuity of the business without financial strain.

To effectively utilize life insurance for tax planning and asset protection, it's important to work with a knowledgeable estate planning attorney or financial advisor. They can assess your specific situation, consider your goals, and help design a life insurance strategy that aligns with your needs and objectives. Additionally, they can provide guidance on tax laws and regulations to ensure compliance and maximize the benefits of life insurance in protecting family assets.

C. Strategies for proper beneficiary designations and preserving wealth for future generations

Proper beneficiary designations are crucial for preserving wealth and ensuring that it passes on to future generations as intended. Here are some strategies to consider:

1. Review Beneficiary Designations Regularly: Life events such as marriage, divorce, birth, or death can impact your intended beneficiaries. Regularly reviewing and updating your beneficiary designations on life insurance policies, retirement accounts, and other assets is essential to ensure that your wealth is distributed according to your wishes.

2. Name Contingent and Successor Beneficiaries: In addition to primary beneficiaries, consider naming contingent beneficiaries who will receive the assets if the primary beneficiary predeceases you. This helps avoid probate and ensures a seamless transfer of wealth. Naming successor beneficiaries can also be beneficial if the primary beneficiary is unable or unwilling to accept the assets.

3. Consider Trusts as Beneficiaries: Establishing a trust and naming it as the beneficiary of your assets can provide added control and protection. Trusts allow you to specify how and when the assets should be distributed to beneficiaries. They can also protect assets from creditors, divorce, and irresponsible spending by future generations.

4. Provide Clear Instructions: When designating beneficiaries, it is essential to provide clear instructions on how you want the assets to be distributed. This can help avoid confusion and potential conflicts among family members. Working with an experienced estate planning attorney can ensure that your intentions are properly documented and legally enforceable.

5. Educate Future Generations: Preserving wealth goes beyond designating beneficiaries. It's important to educate future

generations about financial responsibility, wealth management, and the values associated with the assets they will inherit. By providing financial literacy and guidance, you can help ensure that your wealth is preserved and utilized wisely by future generations.

6. Seek Professional Guidance: Estate planning can be complex, and tax laws are subject to change. Working with a knowledgeable estate planning attorney or financial advisor is crucial to develop a comprehensive plan that aligns with your goals. They can help you navigate legal and tax implications, implement strategies to preserve wealth, and address any unique family dynamics.

Remember, every individual's situation is unique, so it's important to tailor your beneficiary designations and wealth preservation strategies to your specific circumstances. Regularly reviewing and updating your estate plan, along with seeking professional advice, will help ensure that your wealth is effectively preserved and passed on to future generations according to your wishes.

VIII. Real-Life Success Stories

A. Inspiring stories of individuals who have built generational wealth through life insurance despite starting from poverty

Certainly! Here are a few inspiring stories of individuals who have built generational wealth through life insurance, despite starting from poverty:

1. Oprah Winfrey: Oprah grew up in poverty and faced numerous challenges throughout her early life. However, she became one of the most successful media moguls in the world. Life insurance played a crucial role in her journey. When she was a child, her grandmother took out a life insurance policy on her. Even though her grandmother didn't have much money, she recognized the importance of securing Oprah's future. The policy provided a

financial safety net and allowed Oprah to build her empire.

2. Madam C.J. Walker: Madam C.J. Walker was the first female self-made millionaire in the United States. Born to former slaves, she faced poverty and limited opportunities. However, she was determined to create a better life for herself and her daughter. Walker worked as a laundress and eventually started her own hair care business. She not only built a successful company but also purchased life insurance policies to ensure financial security for her daughter and future generations.

3. John H. Johnson: John H. Johnson was the founder of Johnson Publishing Company, which launched Ebony and Jet magazines. Johnson faced poverty and racial discrimination growing up. However, he was determined to succeed and build wealth for his family. Life insurance played a significant role in his success story. When he faced challenges in securing loans from banks, he used his life insurance policies as collateral to fund his business ventures.

4. Sarah Breedlove, also known as Madam C.J. Walker, was an African American entrepreneur and philanthropist. She was the first female self-made millionaire in the United States. Despite being born into poverty, she used her life insurance policy as collateral to start her own hair care business. With dedication and perseverance, she built a successful company and created a legacy of wealth for her family.

These stories highlight how life insurance, combined with determination and entrepreneurship, can help individuals overcome poverty and build generational wealth. It demonstrates the importance of having a financial safety net and the foresight to plan for the future, even when starting from challenging circumstances.

B. Lessons learned and actionable advice from those who have achieved financial prosperity

Here are some lessons learned and actionable advice from individuals who have achieved financial prosperity:

1. Set clear financial goals: Successful individuals understand the importance of setting clear, specific, and achievable financial goals. Whether it's saving a certain amount of money, starting a business, or investing in assets, having goals helps provide direction and motivation.

2. Create a budget and stick to it: Budgeting is a crucial step in managing finances effectively. It allows you to track your income, expenses, and savings. By creating a budget and sticking to it, you gain control over your money and make informed decisions about spending and saving.

3. Invest wisely: Building wealth often involves investing. Successful individuals understand the importance of diversifying their investments and seeking professional advice if needed. They carefully consider different investment options, such as stocks, real estate, or businesses, and make informed decisions based on their risk tolerance, time horizon, and financial goals.

4. Continuous learning and self-improvement: Those who achieve financial prosperity understand the value of ongoing learning. They stay informed about financial matters, industry trends, and investment opportunities. They read books, attend seminars, and seek advice from experts to improve their financial knowledge and make informed decisions.

5. Take calculated risks and embrace failure: Financial success often requires taking calculated risks. Successful individuals understand that failure is a part of the journey and use it as a learning opportunity. They are not afraid to step out of their comfort zone, try new things, and learn from their mistakes.

6. Save and invest early: Time is a valuable asset when it comes to building wealth. Successful individuals emphasize the

importance of starting to save and invest early in life. By starting early, you can take advantage of compounding returns and give your money more time to grow.

7. Build multiple streams of income: Financial prosperity often comes from diversifying income sources. Successful individuals explore various avenues to generate income, such as starting a side business, investing in rental properties, or pursuing passive income opportunities. Having multiple streams of income provides stability and increases the potential for wealth creation.

8. Practice disciplined spending and avoid debt: Financially successful individuals understand the importance of disciplined spending. They prioritize needs over wants, avoid unnecessary debt, and live within their means. They make conscious decisions about their spending and focus on building assets rather than accumulating liabilities.

These lessons and actionable advice can provide valuable guidance for anyone looking to achieve financial prosperity. Remember, everyone's financial journey is unique, and it's important to adapt these lessons to your personal circumstances and goals.

C. Motivation and encouragement for readers to take control of their financial future through life insurance

Taking control of your financial future through life insurance is a smart and responsible step that can provide you and your loved ones with peace of mind. Here's some motivation and encouragement to consider:

1. Protection for your loved ones: Life insurance ensures that your loved ones are financially protected in the event of your untimely passing. It can provide a tax-free lump sum payment to cover funeral expenses, outstanding debts, mortgage payments, and support your family's ongoing financial needs. Knowing that your loved ones will be taken care of can bring you a sense of security

and peace.

2. Income replacement: Life insurance can serve as a source of income replacement for your family. It can help replace lost income, allowing your loved ones to maintain their standard of living and meet their financial obligations. This can provide a safety net during a difficult time and help your family navigate financial challenges without added stress.

3. Debt management: Life insurance can also be used to pay off outstanding debts, such as mortgages, loans, or credit card balances. By having the coverage in place, you can ensure that your loved ones are not burdened with debt after your passing. This can provide them with a fresh start and financial stability.

4. Legacy and inheritance: Life insurance can be a powerful tool for leaving a financial legacy for your loved ones. It can help you create an inheritance that can be used to support your family, fund education for your children, or support charitable causes that are important to you. It allows you to leave a lasting impact beyond your own lifetime.

5. Start early for better rates: Taking control of your financial future through life insurance is best done sooner rather than later. Starting a life insurance policy at a younger age often means lower premiums. By locking in a policy early, you can secure affordable rates and potentially save money over the long term.

6. Flexibility and customization: Life insurance policies come in various forms, such as term life insurance or permanent life insurance. This allows you to choose a policy that aligns with your specific needs and goals. You can customize your coverage amount, policy duration, and even add riders that offer additional benefits, such as critical illness coverage or disability protection.

Remember, life insurance is a long-term commitment that requires careful consideration and evaluation of your financial situation. It's always advisable to consult with a financial advisor or insurance professional who can guide you through the process and help you make an informed decision based on your unique circumstances.

By taking control of your financial future through life insurance, you're making a proactive choice to protect your loved ones and build a solid foundation for their future.

IX. Empowering Financial Education

A. The importance of financial literacy for the underprivileged community

Financial literacy is crucial for everyone, especially for underprivileged communities. Here are some reasons why financial literacy is important for the underprivileged community:

1. Empowerment and independence: Financial literacy empowers individuals to make informed decisions about their money. It equips them with the knowledge and skills needed to manage their finances effectively, enabling them to take control of their financial future. By understanding basic financial concepts, budgeting, saving, and managing debt, individuals in underprivileged communities can become more self-reliant, reducing their reliance on external financial support.

2. Breaking the cycle of poverty: Financial literacy can play a significant role in breaking the cycle of poverty. By equipping individuals with the knowledge and skills to make sound financial decisions, they can better navigate economic challenges and improve their financial well-being. Understanding concepts such as budgeting, saving, and investing can help individuals in underprivileged communities make the most of their limited resources, potentially leading to increased savings, improved economic stability, and better opportunities for upward mobility.

3. Building financial resilience: Financial literacy helps

individuals in underprivileged communities build resilience against financial shocks and emergencies. By understanding the importance of emergency funds and insurance, they can better prepare for unexpected expenses and mitigate the impact of financial setbacks. This can prevent them from falling into debt traps or resorting to predatory lending practices, which often disproportionately affect underprivileged communities.

4. Access to financial services: Financial literacy can improve access to financial services for underprivileged communities. By understanding how banking works, the importance of credit scores, and the benefits of saving and investing, individuals can become more confident and knowledgeable consumers. This can open doors to better banking services, affordable loans, and other financial products that can help them build assets and improve their financial situation.

5. Entrepreneurship and economic growth: Financial literacy can foster entrepreneurship and economic growth within underprivileged communities. By understanding the fundamentals of business finance, individuals can make informed decisions about starting and managing their own businesses. This can create opportunities for economic self-sufficiency, job creation, and overall community development.

6. Long-term financial planning: Financial literacy encourages long-term financial planning, which is essential for building wealth and achieving financial goals. By understanding concepts such as investing, retirement planning, and estate planning, individuals in underprivileged communities can work towards a more secure and prosperous future. This can help break the cycle of generational poverty and create a foundation for sustainable economic growth.

Efforts should be made to provide accessible and culturally relevant financial education programs tailored to the specific needs of underprivileged communities. By equipping individuals with the necessary financial knowledge and skills, we can empower them to make informed decisions, improve their financial well-being, and create a brighter future for themselves and their communities.

B. Resources and tools to enhance financial knowledge and capability

There are several resources and tools available to enhance financial knowledge and capability. Here are a few:

1. Online courses and educational websites: Many reputable organizations and institutions offer free or affordable online courses on various financial topics. Websites like Coursera, Udemy, and Khan Academy provide courses on personal finance, investing, budgeting, and more. These courses often include interactive modules and quizzes to test your understanding.

2. Financial literacy apps: There are numerous mobile apps designed to improve financial literacy. Apps like Mint, YNAB (You Need a Budget), and PocketGuard help track expenses, create budgets, and set financial goals. They provide insights and reminders to help users make better financial decisions.

3. Government and non-profit resources: Governments and non-profit organizations often provide financial education resources and tools. National or local government websites may offer free guides, calculators, and workshops on topics such as budgeting, saving, and debt management. Non-profit organizations like the National Endowment for Financial Education (NEFE) and the Financial Literacy and Education Commission (FLEC) also offer valuable resources.

4. Community workshops and seminars: Local community centers, libraries, and non-profit organizations often host workshops and seminars on financial literacy. These sessions provide opportunities to learn from experts and ask questions in a supportive environment. Check for events in your area or inquire

with local organizations for upcoming workshops.

5. Books and podcasts: There is a wide range of books and podcasts available on personal finance and financial literacy. Some popular titles include "Rich Dad Poor Dad" by Robert Kiyosaki, "The Total Money Makeover" by Dave Ramsey, and "Your Money or Your Life" by Vicki Robin. Podcasts like "The Dave Ramsey Show" and "ChooseFI" offer valuable insights and advice on financial topics.

6. Financial literacy games: Interactive games can be a fun and engaging way to learn about finance. Games like "Money Metropolis" and "Financial Football" are designed to teach financial concepts while keeping users entertained. They can be particularly useful for teaching children and young adults about money management.

Remember, it's important to choose reputable sources and tailor the resources to your specific needs and goals. By utilizing these resources and tools, you can enhance your financial knowledge and capability, ultimately leading to better financial decision-making and improved financial well-being.

C. Practical tips for making informed financial decisions and achieving long-term prosperity

Here are some practical tips to help you make informed financial decisions and achieve long-term prosperity:

1. Set clear financial goals: Define your short-term and long-term financial goals. This could include saving for a down payment on a house, paying off debt, or building an emergency fund. Having specific goals will help you stay focused and make decisions aligned with your objectives.

2. Create a budget: Develop a realistic budget that tracks your income and expenses. This will give you a clear picture of where your money is going and help you identify areas where you can cut back or save. Be sure to allocate funds for savings and

investments as well.

3. Educate yourself: Take the time to learn about personal finance and investment strategies. Read books, attend workshops, or listen to podcasts on topics like budgeting, investing, and retirement planning. The more knowledge you have, the better equipped you'll be to make informed decisions.

4. Minimize debt: Aim to reduce and manage your debt responsibly. Prioritize paying off high-interest debts first, such as credit cards or personal loans. Consider consolidating your debts or negotiating lower interest rates to make repayment more manageable.

5. Build an emergency fund: Set aside money in an emergency fund to cover unexpected expenses, such as medical bills or car repairs. Aim to save three to six months' worth of living expenses in a separate account that is easily accessible.

6. Diversify your investments: Don't put all your eggs in one basket. Diversify your investment portfolio across different asset classes, such as stocks, bonds, and real estate. This helps spread risk and increases the potential for long-term growth.

7. Plan for retirement: Start saving for retirement as early as possible. Contribute to retirement accounts like 401(k)s or IRAs and take advantage of employer matching programs. Consider consulting with a financial advisor to ensure you have a solid retirement plan in place.

8. Review insurance coverage: Regularly review your insurance policies to ensure you have adequate coverage. This includes health insurance, life insurance, disability insurance, and homeowner's or renter's insurance. Make adjustments as necessary to protect yourself and your assets.

9. Avoid impulse spending: Before making a purchase, take the time to evaluate if it aligns with your financial goals and if it's a

necessary expense. Avoid impulsive buying and practice delaying gratification when possible.

10. Regularly review and adjust your financial plan: Life circumstances and financial goals can change over time, so it's important to review your financial plan regularly. Make adjustments as needed to stay on track and continue working towards long-term prosperity.

By following these practical tips, you'll be better equipped to make informed financial decisions, improve your financial well-being, and work towards long-term prosperity. Remember, it's a journey, and consistency and discipline are key.

X. Conclusion

A. Recap of key concepts and strategies discussed in the book

Here's a recap of key concepts and strategies discussed in the book about building wealth through life insurance:

1. Permanent life insurance: The book suggests considering permanent life insurance policies, such as whole life or universal life. Unlike term life insurance, permanent policies provide coverage for the insured's entire life and can accumulate cash value over time.

2. Cash value accumulation: Permanent life insurance policies have a cash value component that grows over time. The book advises leveraging this cash value to build wealth by utilizing policy loans or withdrawals for various purposes, such as investing in real estate, starting a business, or funding education.

3. Tax advantages: The book highlights the tax advantages of permanent life insurance. The cash value growth within the policy is tax-deferred, meaning you won't have to pay taxes on the gains until you withdraw them. Additionally, death benefits are typically income tax-free for beneficiaries.

4. Flexibility and control: Permanent life insurance policies offer flexibility and control over the cash value. The book recommends choosing policies that allow for flexible premium payments, adjusting death benefit amounts, and accessing cash value when needed.

5. Estate planning: Life insurance can play a crucial role in estate planning. The book suggests using life insurance proceeds to cover estate taxes, provide for loved ones, or leave a legacy for future generations.

6. Regular policy review: The book emphasizes the importance of regularly reviewing your life insurance policy to ensure it aligns with your changing financial goals and circumstances. Adjustments may be necessary as your income, family situation, or financial objectives evolve.

7. Risk management: Life insurance serves as a risk management tool. The book suggests evaluating your needs for life insurance coverage based on factors such as dependents, outstanding debts, and financial obligations. Having adequate coverage can provide peace of mind and protect your loved ones in the event of your passing.

8. Working with a financial advisor: The book advises seeking guidance from a qualified financial advisor when considering life insurance as a wealth-building strategy. An advisor can help assess your specific needs, recommend suitable policies, and provide ongoing support.

It's important to note that the strategies discussed in the book are specific to using life insurance as a wealth-building tool. As with any financial decision, it's essential to carefully evaluate the pros and cons, consider your individual circumstances, and consult with professionals before implementing any strategy.

B. Encouragement to take action and leverage life insurance as

a means to build generational wealth

Building generational wealth is an important goal, and leveraging life insurance can be a powerful tool to help you achieve it. Here's some encouragement to take action:

1. Start now: Time is a valuable asset when it comes to building wealth. The sooner you start leveraging life insurance, the longer your cash value and death benefit have to grow. So don't wait - take action today!

2. Think long-term: Building generational wealth requires a long-term mindset. Life insurance policies, especially permanent ones, are designed to provide coverage and accumulate cash value over a lifetime. By embracing this long-term perspective, you can maximize the benefits for yourself and future generations.

3. Educate yourself: Take the time to educate yourself about the different types of life insurance policies, their benefits, and how they can be used to build wealth. The more you understand, the better equipped you'll be to make informed decisions and take advantage of the opportunities life insurance offers.

4. Consult with professionals: Seek guidance from financial advisors and insurance professionals who specialize in life insurance and wealth-building strategies. They can help you assess your unique financial situation, goals, and risk tolerance, and provide personalized recommendations to help you leverage life insurance effectively.

5. Review your existing policies: If you already have life insurance, review your policies to ensure they align with your current goals. If necessary, consider adjusting your coverage or exploring additional options that better suit your wealth-building objectives.

6. Create a plan: Develop a comprehensive financial plan that incorporates life insurance as a key component of your wealth-

building strategy. Set specific goals, outline the steps you need to take, and regularly review and update your plan as circumstances change.

7. Take advantage of tax benefits: Remember that life insurance offers tax advantages, such as tax-deferred growth and potentially tax-free death benefits. By leveraging these benefits, you can optimize your wealth-building potential.

8. Teach future generations: Share your knowledge and experiences with your loved ones. Educate them about the benefits of life insurance and the importance of building generational wealth. By passing on this knowledge, you empower future generations to continue the legacy you've started.

Remember, building generational wealth takes time, discipline, and a strategic approach. By leveraging life insurance as a means to accumulate wealth, you can create a solid foundation for the financial well-being of your family for years to come. So, take action, stay committed, and watch your wealth grow across generations.

C. Inspiring readers to break free from the cycle of poverty and leave a lasting legacy for future generations

Breaking free from the cycle of poverty and leaving a lasting legacy for future generations is an inspiring and empowering goal. Here's some encouragement to help you on this journey:

1. Believe in your potential: Remember that your circumstances do not define your worth or limit your potential. With determination, hard work, and a positive mindset, you can overcome the challenges of poverty and create a better future for yourself and your family.

2. Education is key: Invest in your education and skills development. Education is a powerful tool that can open doors to new opportunities, higher-paying jobs, and a brighter future.

Take advantage of scholarships, grants, and vocational training programs to enhance your knowledge and skills.

3. Set clear goals: Define your goals and create a roadmap to achieve them. Whether it's starting a business, pursuing higher education, or acquiring assets, having clear goals gives you direction and motivation. Break them down into smaller, actionable steps to make them more attainable.

4. Develop financial literacy: Educate yourself about personal finance and money management. Learn about budgeting, saving, investing, and building credit. By acquiring financial knowledge, you can make informed decisions, avoid debt traps, and grow your wealth over time.

5. Build a support network: Surround yourself with positive and supportive individuals who believe in your aspirations. Seek out mentors, join community groups, or connect with organizations that offer resources and support for individuals looking to break free from poverty. Their guidance and encouragement can be invaluable on your journey.

6. Embrace entrepreneurship: Consider starting your own business or pursuing self-employment opportunities. Entrepreneurship offers the potential for financial independence and the ability to create jobs for others. Take advantage of resources and programs that support small businesses and provide mentorship for aspiring entrepreneurs.

7. Invest in assets: Look for opportunities to invest in assets that appreciate over time, such as real estate, stocks, or businesses. Investing wisely can generate passive income and build wealth that can be passed down to future generations.

8. Teach financial literacy to future generations: Break the cycle of poverty by equipping future generations with financial knowledge and skills. Teach your children about budgeting, saving, and investing, and instill in them the importance of

education and hard work. By empowering them with financial literacy, you set them on a path towards financial success.

Remember, breaking free from the cycle of poverty and leaving a lasting legacy requires determination, perseverance, and a long-term mindset. Believe in yourself, seek opportunities for growth, and never stop learning. By taking these steps, you can create a better future for yourself, your family, and generations to come.

Dear readers,

Thank you for taking the time to explore the idea of breaking free from the cycle of poverty and leaving a lasting legacy for future generations. Your commitment to personal growth and resilience is truly inspiring.

We would greatly appreciate it if you could share your thoughts and experiences with us by leaving an honest review. Your feedback is invaluable in helping us improve and create content that resonates with you. By sharing your thoughts, you are not only helping us but also empowering others who may be on a similar journey.

Thank you once again for being a part of our community. We look forward to hearing from you and continuing to provide support and inspiration.

Warm regards,
Mark Livingston